Ask No Questions

Ask No Questions

(a migrant's tale)

Eva Collins

PUNCHER & WATTMANN

First published in 2022
Published by Puncher and Wattmann
PO Box 279
Waratah NSW 2298

https://www.puncherandwattmann.com
web@puncherandwattmann.com

ISBN   9781922571342

Cover design by Miranda Douglas and Eva Collins
Typesetting by Morgan Arnett
Printed by Lightning Source International

A catalogue record for this work is available from the National Library of Australia

Supported by a City of Melbourne Arts Grant.

In memory of my parents,
Rena and Joe Skovell

About the Author

Eva Collins was born in Poland and came to Australia with her family in 1958. She holds Bachelor degrees in Philosophy (University of Melbourne) and Fine Art Photography (RMIT), as well as a Master's degree in Contemporary Art (Victorian College of the Arts).

Eva was a finalist in the Olive Cotton and Moran Portrait Awards, and won the Inaugural Nikon Prize (2005). Her photographs are held at the National Portrait Gallery and the State Library of Victoria among other places, and have been widely exhibited. Her short videos have been shown at various film festivals and have won awards.

Her poems have appeared in *Best Australian Poems*, *Quadrant*, *Southerly* and *Westerly*. An extract from this collection was first published in the *Newcastle Poetry Prize Anthology* (2008).

Acknowledgements

I wish to thank the City of Melbourne for not only receiving my family and me as migrants, but also for awarding me a grant which greatly helped with the publishing of this memoir.

Special thanks to Jordie Albiston who has edited my manuscript and showed so much enthusiasm for my work.

I am grateful to Gemma Dean-Furlong, Anne Carson, Jodie Webster, Erica Wagner, Coral Huckstep and Dr Haas Dellal for their warm support and encouragement.

Instead of looking at things, look between things.

John Baldessari

Children are silent witnesses to the dramas that shape our times. They are the forgotten child citizens.

Kirsty Murray

Preface

Ask No Questions is a record of my family's immigration from communist Poland to Australia during the Cold War in the late 1950s. It is told from my perspective as a twelve-year-old girl, who was heartbroken about leaving her mother country.

The poetry is restrained and spare, which mirrors the caution, alertness and fear my parents felt living under a surveillance regime and amid anti-Semitism.

The transitions of migration are rarely easy or straightforward. You gain something and you lose something in the process. By leaving your country, you leave behind treasured things which helped form your identity. In your new country, this identity becomes vulnerable as the usual reference points are not there. Just as the migrants are foreigners to the Australians, so too it is the Australians who are foreign to the migrants.

Aside from telling my own story, the theme of this collection applies to all migrants and refugees from anywhere and at any time. *Ask No Questions* endeavors to elicit empathy and understanding for people on the other side of a divide. It is also laced with humor, which I hope offers some welcome comic relief.

Contents

Prologue

Form

Surname

       Collins, double 'l'
with a stroke of a pen I go
from Kovalski
to conformity.

First Name

       Eva
the only remnant of faraway lands
where seasons are back to front.

DOB

       20 January 1946
it should have been February
I came early
with the cord around my neck.

Place of Birth

       Poland
the hospital in ruins

Address

       Leafy suburbia
       swimming pool in the backyard
no sign of struggle here
picture-perfect.

<u>Signature</u>

       Which name?
the one that endured danger
or this one
ordinary and safe?

My pen dries up.

Departure

Suitcases

Warsaw, 1958

I don't know why we are leaving.
My parents tell me to pack my things.
      Ask no questions.

I pack my favourite books,
locks of friends' hair,
a few grains of Polish soil folded into a lace handkerchief.

Mum and Dad pack volumes of poetry
political jokes
memories of laughter,

slam the lid shut
on police doorknocks
redacted mail.

Ela—Why are you leaving?
Tomek—Will you come back?
Basia starts to cry.

I have no answers.

I plant a chestnut in our courtyard
to leave something of me behind.

Departure

January 1958

At the train station
the icy air pricks
our faces.

At minus twenty degrees
our friends huddle like penguins
against the lashing wind.

Through misted breaths they chorus—
Long live the Kovalskis!
May we live to see you again.

They wipe tears
throw streamers and flowers
for good luck.

Journey

Journey

The train
rushes us off
into the black night.

I am wrenched from:
      best friends
      red rattling trams
      barrels of herring
      light fluffy cheesecakes
      sweet-smelling bagels
      frozen sausages
      hanging from windows in snow
      statues of Socialist heroes
      watching over me
      making me feel safe.

I am sobbing.
Dad—You'll come back when you're older.
Me—I'll be someone else then.

Midnight

Border guards thump the train walls
shine torches beneath its carriages.
Alsatian dogs sniff for anyone
clutching the underbelly.

My parents tell me
sometimes people hide there.
It's their only way
out of Poland.

Me—What if they fall off?
Dad—Ask no questions.

I wonder why
gold broaches are pinned
to my underwear
to my brother's nappies.

Mum—Ask no questions.

I wonder why
a barrel of butter
is standing broad-hipped
in the passageway.

A knock at our door.

From the top bunk
I see Dad
hand over his passport
with some bank notes inside.

The guard
slides the money
into his breast pocket
salutes and leaves.

Austria I
January 1958

We reach Vienna.
Mum and Dad embrace
skol a shot of vodka.

I weep.
I have lost
everything.

They say we left the Iron Curtain behind.
What iron curtain?
I didn't see any curtains!

Mum—It describes countries
ruled by iron-fisted leaders.
who punish anyone who criticises them.

Me—But if Poland is that bad
why aren't all our friends
leaving too?

Mum—It's not easy
to start life all over again.

Dad—I don't want you
to experience anti-Semitism.

I don't know what that means.

Dad—It means prejudice
against the Jews.
I am Jewish.

Me—Dad, you killed Jesus!

He blinks and shakes his head.
Dear child, I've never even met the man!

Austria II

In Vienna, at the Hotel Edelweiss
Mum and Dad roll up their sleeves
and squelch through the butter in the barrel.

One by one
greasy glittering gems
emerge out of hiding.

Afterwards they unfasten
the jewellery on
my baby brother and me.

Dad—portable investments.
We'll sell these
in Australia.

I learn we were only allowed
to take food with us and twenty American dollars.
Valuables had to be left behind.

On a park bench
a mother peels an orange
for her little boy.

Oranges

In Poland
oranges were forbidden at school
so children who could not afford such luxury
would not feel bad.

If someone secretly brought this exotic fruit
we sat mesmerised
as the waft of its scent
gave the owner away.

Italy

February 1958

In Bologna the Italians
move their hands excitedly
when they speak.

They make funny faces
at Robert, my little brother.
Call him *Bello Bambino*.

I want to stay in this cheerful place.
Dad—No, safety from Moscow
lies further away.

We take a boat to Australia.

Boat
May 1958

Stuck for one month
nothing but a vast grey ocean.

Afloat between:
>continents
>time-zones
>memories
>fantasies.

Moisture covers railings
deckchairs and walls.
Everything is sticky
the air is stuffy.

Dining tables are
fixed to the floor.
When the boat rolls
the chairs slide away
to the other side of the room.

Soup spills.
Plates crash.
People scream.

When it's quiet again
we walk the decks
try to talk to people
whose languages are different to ours.

We stop at various ports.

When we dock in Colombo
hawkers sail up to our boat

throw ropes over the railings
weighted with baskets
of local produce.

We buy wooden carvings
woven rugs
embroidered scarves
and fruit.

I've never seen a pineapple before.
I've never seen black people before.
I want to go down
and touch their silky skin.

I wonder what my life will be like in Australia.

Will I have a pet koala?
Will I have Aboriginal friends?
Do they grow oranges there?

Australia

Australia I
June 1958

We dock at Port Melbourne
grim, dark, deserted.

No streamers
no flowers to welcome us.
Have we come to the wrong place?

Friends who sponsored us
pretending to be family
drive us to their home
on the left side of the road!

We sit down to steak, chips and tinned peas.
I've never had tinned peas before.
In Warsaw I had to shell them.

I've never seen wall-to-wall carpets.
In Warsaw we had rugs
on parquetry floors.

In their bathroom the shower rose
is fixed to the ceiling.
In Warsaw we had a hand-held one.

They show us a shed
which shelters their Holden
and out the back
a field of grass.

Everyone's dream.
A block of land in the suburbs.

I wonder if this is where they will graze sheep.

Summer

We're staying
in a rooming-house
in St Kilda.

Ice-cream melts.
It runs down my fingers
before I finish it.

There is no breeze.
The air is a thick pillow
smothering my face.

I stick my head
into an open fridge
to escape the heat.

St Kilda I

Blinding light
strafes the asphalt.
Shade and shadow
offer some relief.
Even the flowers seem bleached.

Everything is shielded:
      low roofs on houses
      verandas over shop windows
      men's eyes concealed
      beneath broad hat brims.

The streets are empty.
We look around.
The only things moving
are the trees' shadows.
Mum—Are we the only living beings here?

Beginnings

The Aussies are friendly
but not interested in our history.
Forget your past. You must blend in.

Dad now dresses
like the other office workers.
Long shorts and high white socks.

Cooling off knee caps
seems the only concession
to hot weather.

He trudges with his suitcase
bulging with samples
tablecloths, placemats, tea towels.

Up and down Flinders Lane
(the Schmate District).
to the city wholesalers.

He changes our name to Collins.
Teaches Mum
how to pronounce it.

Milkbar

In Mr Stewart's grocery store
I meet Ania.

She's my age and also Polish.
I'm drawn to her straightaway.

We talk about feathery snowflakes
tickling our tongues.

The fragrance
of linden tree blossoms.

Horse hooves
clopping on cobblestones.

Lady customer—Speak English!
I don't know what you're saying!

Mr Stewart—You don't have to know
what they're saying.

The lady storms out.

Street

We move to Caulfield
a little house in the suburbs.

The little houses have little gardens in front
and bigger ones at the back.

On Sundays men push mowers to and fro
proud when their lawns look like green velvet.

My mother brings our next-door neighbor
the prize tomato from our vegetable patch

Neighbour—Good onya, love.
We wonder if he's been drinking.
Why would he call the tomato an onion?

School

I'm in Form 2.
Miss Taylor asks us to dust the bookshelves.
Why would she want us to do that?
They're already dusty!

Looking at a photo of Mount Kościuszko
I tell the class it's pronounced
Mount *Koshchooshko*
named after the Polish freedom fighter.

Miss Taylor—That's not how we say it here, Eva.

Maureen asks to share her lunch with me.
Says her mother has packed
some nice hot dogs.
I'm nearly sick when she says that.

Lorraine makes fun
of my accent.
She pretends to talk like me
makes ugly faces.

Lorraine—Go back to where you came from.
That's nice of her to see I miss Poland.
Me—Thank you, I wish I could.
She screws up her face.

Fight

After class
I accidentally drop my key
at the lockers.

Lorraine stamps on it
and won't budge.

I say in my best English—
Please remove your foot.

She hisses—
Make me!

I don't understand.
How can I make her?
She is made already.

      A language whiteout.
I gently push her foot.
The next thing there are
      clumps of hair
      splotches of blood
and this feeling
of going for it at an
accelerating
exhilarating
speed.
  Punch! Pinch! Pull!
  Scrape! Scratch! Spit!

The headmistress pins me against the wall.
You're suspended for two days!

I'm terrified of what my parents will say.

Dad nods—Sometimes it's important
to stand up for yourself.

Mum—Better to use words
than fists.

Strap

I am talking in class.
Mr Gronow calls me to his desk.
Tells me to stick out my hand.
Takes a leather strap.

Just as the strap comes down
I pull my hand back.
He frowns, grabs my hand
and brings the strap down again.

My hand burns.
My eyes smart.
How can such warm soft fingers
deliver so much pain?

Reminiscence I

Warsaw 1957

School assembly years back.
Visiting Soviet teachers on the podium
look at us looking at them.
We sing a Russian song
without a clue what the words mean.

Afterwards we call out in one voice—
Long Live Polish-Soviet Friendship!
Tomek whispers loudly
Only if we do what the Ruskis tell us!

The next day his parents
are summoned to school.
Dire consequences will follow
if Tomek does that again.

After that their flat is wire-tapped.

Funtimes

Maureen
her friend Jill
Ania and I

take the green rattling tram
to the movies
on Saturdays.

Jill—How old are you?
Me—I am twelve years of age.
But I'm not old.

We snack on Anzac biscuits
watch cartoons.
Laugh our heads off.

I say—Good-onya, love
and right-ee-o.
Hope I sound convincing.

Christmas
December 1960

Christmas lunch is at Jill's.
The invitation says
Mr and Mrs James Brown
cordially invite you to our home
for a barbecue.

Me—Gosh.
I didn't know
your mum's first name
was the same as your dad's.
Jill laughs—It's not!

I introduce my parents.
Dad kisses Jill's mother's hand
I nearly die of embarrassment.
So does Jill's mother
I think.

Grilled sausages
and salad are followed by
a hundred helpings
of mouth-watering
pavlova.

My parents bring
herring in oil
and Kugelhopf cake.
The cake is gone in no time
but the herring stays on.

Tea

Maureen's parents invite us
for tea.
They call us
the New Australians.

We eat dinner at home
before heading there
for cups of tea.

When we arrive
the table is set for dinner!

Feigning hunger
we ask for second helpings.

In time Mum says she's happy
but wherever she goes
her shadow stays behind.

St Kilda II

On Sundays
my parents meet their Polish friends
on St Kilda Beach.

Dad shakes hands with
Franek, Marek, Yanek.
Starts a discussion on business and politics.

Mum kisses Bella, Fela, Hela.
Out comes the coconut butter
for that golden Hawaiian tan.

Men with their chests puffed out
swoop on women
who need a light.

Women squeezed into swimsuits
parade like seals along the pier.
Avoid men's eyes diving into their cleavages.

They dip their toes in the water
then swim breaststroke
not to smudge their mascara.

They wear rubber caps with quivering flowers
each thinking they're the next
Esther Williams.

Only Fellini is missing.

Scheherazade

In the evening
we stroll to Café Scheherazade
our European haven
in Acland Street.

When our friends
come together
they are doctors, lawyers, engineers
again.

No longer
storemen, assembly line workers, waiters
as they are in Australia
during the day.

They joke, laugh, advise.
Take comfort in:
>pickled herring
>sauerkraut
>schnitzel
>horseradish
>Black Forest
>and poppy seed cake.

Food that reminds them
of home.
Food that makes me feel cosy
inside.

Nightclub

Afterwards, those who have the strength
troop off to Elwood's Moulin Rouge.
My parents drag me with them.

Alex Stern: ex-surgeon, now shopkeeper	bongos
Leo Rosner: saved by Schindler	accordion
Kuba Berkovski: judge, now waiter	piano
Lilka 'La Lolo': teacher, now machinist	croons 'Hernando's Hideaway'

Women
in body-hugging dresses
flutter their eyelashes.

Men
slick their hair
approach the women to dance.

Couples shuffle foxtrot
cheek-to-cheek
hoping to ignite desire
numb fatigue.

By midnight
drunk and sweaty
they stagger out.

Pray they'll pull through
another sixty-hour week.

Reminiscence II

In Warsaw every Sunday
we met friends at the Hotel Bristol.

The café brimmed with
clouds of cigarette smoke
waves of coffee aroma
sweet-smelling hazelnut cakes.

Maestro, tuxedoed with waxed moustache,
zipped his fingers across the keyboard.
Someone started to sing.
Mum recited poetry.

Men bowed greeting other men.
Kissed women's hands.

Red lip-sticked ladies
kissed me in turn
then rubbed smudges
off my cheeks.

Told me how much I've grown
though they saw me every week.

Evenings

Sometimes Mum looks at photographs
and weeps.

Mum—We're so far from
Europe.

Me—Let's go back to Poland
where life is normal.

My little brother—
What is Poland?

Dad—We've burnt our bridges there.
We're safe and free here.

But I don't feel free at all.
Everything is strange.

The eucalypts smell lovely
but they don't change with the seasons.

The possums are cute
but they're only pretend squirrels.

Christmas in summer
feels fake.

Reminscence III

Winter hushed in
blanketed roofs and trees in plush snow
sculpted icicles
which we broke off and licked.

At night the snow sparkled in silvery moonlight
and crunched under our feet.
Our caretaker pooled water from the hose at night.
By morning the ice rink was set.

The kids from our flats ran down to skate.
Afterwards we built a snowman
watched it melt
when the sun came out.

Parents

My father takes pride
in jobs well done
but can't fix
Mum's melancholy.

Dad—Don't look back.
We must be strong.
If we trip and fall
all will be lost.

Mum gulps down spirits
to prop up her own
then bloated with brandy
spills soup on the floor.

She holds back her tears
which turn into blisters
bulging and bursting
all over her face.

She takes a hot iron
and melts a wry smile
peeling her skin
back to raw flesh.

And when she screams
only the strays stop to listen.
Losing her grip
it's the drunks who catch her fall.

Dad—Cherish your freedom.
Forget the past.
Mum—Yes, yes.
Forget the past.

She goes to her room
pulls down the blinds
turns on the TV
turns off the sound.

Reminiscence IV

At home my parents
whispered with their friends
sent me out of the room
closed the door.
Listened to a scratchy radio broadcast.

Why don't you dial a clear station? I called out.

Ask no questions.

Comfort

We still have:
       packets of
       dried mushrooms
       bags of
       buckwheat
       jars of
       sauerkraut
brought with us from Poland.

I cook a meal
pretend I'm fed
by my mother
country.

Homecoming

Reclaim

December 1964

I am back
in Poland.

I've come to reclaim:
      herringbone parquetry
      tea served in glasses
      held in silver cradles
      sour milk
      with dill and radishes
      plump cheesecake
      tasting as it should
      an alphabet
      written with serifs
my lost years.

At the airport
I sneak in *Animal Farm*
under my blouse.

My friends asked for this book.
Banned in Poland.
It is too similar to what goes on there.

Before I leave Australia
I plant a gumnut in my backyard.
To leave something of me behind.

Warsaw

The red trams still rattle.
The cheesecake is fluffy.
The hill in the park is now smaller
my old friends are taller.

They want to meet me
in an open park
in case their homes
are bugged.

I bring them each
supersize boxes of chocolate
and a few oranges
so expensive here.

Tomek's voice is deeper.
Ela's hair is darker.
Basia is still bubbly.
They want to visit me in Australia.

Homecoming

Basia and Ela
put their arms around me—
Stay with us Eva!
Don't leave us again!

I go inside my old school.
It still smells of the same floor polish.
I am buoyed
by its familiarity.

I see a new basketball court.
The old library is gone.
The old school uniforms
have changed.

I want to say hello
to my dear old teachers
I look around
but don't see any faces I know.

Tree I

I visit my old flat.
The people who live there
invite me in
for cake and tea.

They ask about life in Australia.
Are the summers very hot?
Do kangaroos hop
in city parks?

It's still my flat
but it feels like
strangers
have trespassed.

I look out the old window
and smile to see
a new tall linden tree
growing.

Tree II

I remember
the day
our living room
seemed much brighter.

The old tree
that shaded our window
had been cut down.

Inside the birdhouse
nailed to its trunk
Dad kept a bag
of American dollars
forbidden at the time
in Poland.

Afraid that the police
were hiding in wait
he never retrieved
the bag.

Longing

My chestnut is already a sapling.
I open my water bottle
give it a little drink.

Out of my neighbour's open window
I breathe in the aroma of chicken soup
hear strains of a Chopin mazurka.
I stop and cry.

Everyone speaks Polish here:
       not just at home
       but in the tram
       on the streets
       in the shops
without lowering their voices.

Little children speak it better than me!

Letter

Dear Dad,

I'm in *Senatorska Street*
facing the flat you once lived in
before the war.

Before
the Germans enclosed it
in the Ghetto.

Before
you became a hunted man.

Did you sense then what was in store for you?

I'm looking at what you looked at when you stepped out of your flat.
You would have looked at these stately buildings,
crossed the verdant Saski Gardens.
Did the trams rumble the same way?
Did you go into the canteen around the corner
boasting the best home-made borscht in town?

I'm in here now.
I've ordered borscht.
It's sprinkled with dill
just as you make it
back in Melbourne.

Sooty chimney sweepers walk
past the window.
I grab the button on my blouse
hold my breath.
For good luck.
You'd have laughed
had you been here with me.

I wish you were.

Dear Mum

I'm in the foyer of
the *Syrena Theatre*
where you performed before we left.

There is chatter
peals of laughter
wafts of perfume.

The bell rings.
Patrons butt out cigarettes
rush in to see the show.
The way they rushed
to see you on stage.

You should be here.
You loved the limelight.

You lost all this.
I'm so sorry.

Now you wait alone
on a sunbaked street
for the slow tram to
take you from the sleepy suburbs
to the City where there are voices.

Poland

I eat Poland
drink Poland
breathe Poland in.

Wherever I go
it goes with me.

I see it—it looks at me.
I hear it—it speaks to me.
I smell it—it surrounds me.
I say it—it talks back to me.
I touch it and it touches me back.

I take a tram
get jostled with others.

I stand in a queue
buy biały ser with kminek
Wedel chocolates
a litre of vodka
take them to friends'
for lunch.

I go to an outdoor concert.
I merge into the crowd.
You can't tell me apart
from the others.

Changes

Everything is familiar
and yet different.
Am I in a dream?

Grandpas pull grandkids on sleds.
From time to time they stop
and have a snowball fight.

My uncle and aunt serve pierogi
my favourite dumplings
topped with dill and kefir.

They won't let me walk barefoot
in their apartment.
They say—You'll catch a cold.

Back in Melbourne
I never wear slippers
indoors.

They ask
if we want to come back
are we happy we left?

My parents left Poland
because of the bad
despite the good.

I've come back
for the good
despite the bad.

I'm here
on borrowed time.
I don't want to leave.

I get a postcard from Jill:
I miss you, come back soon!
Maureen got into swimming squad!
Ania asks for a pressed Polish flower.

Return

Australia II

January 1965

At the airport
my parents and I
run towards each other.

I hear—BOO!
and there behind them
are Maureen, Jill, Ania.

We hug
until we fall over.
They ask about my trip.

They make me promise
to take them with me
next time I go.

My parents
bombard me with
a million questions.

Mum says she likes her job
as a make-up artist *but*
it's not the same as performing in theatre.

Dad now plays golf—It's a fun game.

My brother says—Cześć
for hello in Polish.

Unlike me
he has no accent
when he speaks English.

Socialising

My friends and I go bodysurfing
practice rock-n-roll moves
lose our voices
at football matches.

I take them to the local synagogue
which holds dances on Saturday nights.

Chubby Checker and the Twist
is all the rage.
One word from his mouth
sends our bunch into
wild dancing.

The best of us do it on one foot.
Some lose their balance
twist their ankles
and fall.

That night
wanting to impress a boy
I keep going full-blast.
Then the music slows down.

Everyone stops.
But I keep going.

Aware all eyes are on me
I add the occasional sidekick
to spice up my moves.

The boy I like
taps me on my shoulder.
He says—You're dancing
to Israel's national anthem.

Me—Right…
I beg for the floor to open
and swallow me up.

Ania, Jill and Maureen stand in front of me
so I don't have to face the crowd.

Next day we meet at the beach
eat ice-cream
and laugh about the night before.

Belonging

I still miss Warsaw
and when in Warsaw
I miss Melbourne.

It's hard to be
in two places at once.

I hear 'Crying in the Rain'
and my eyes
well up with tears.

Maureen—It's good
to have you home
Eva Collins.

Me—It's good to be here
with you guys
but from now on
I am Eva *Kovalski*-Collins.

.

Epilogue

If

my parents had never left Poland—

my Greek husband
would have lived too far away
for us to meet

my children would not be
my children

possums would be squirrels
and dingoes wolves

Christmas would be white
night would be day

I would garnish our dinner
with pyetrooshka
not parsley
and laugh at how
Mount Koshchooshko
is called *Kozeeosko*

I'd holiday on the Amber
not the Gold Coast
drink vodka
not whiskey
make passionate love to Sigmund
not Keith or Wayne.

If my parents had never left Poland
maybe I'd wonder
what I'd be like
if they had.

Notes

- Australia's highest mountain was named after General Kościuszko in 1840 by the Polish explorer, Paul Edmund Strzelecki. Thaddeus Kościuszko was an 18th century freedom fighter who fought in Poland against the Russians and in the USA against the British. After many years of having the name spelled incorrectly, finally in 1998 'z' and an acute accent over the first 's' was added by the NSW Geographical Names Board.

- The Cold War is a name given to the period between 1947 and 1991. It was a time when the Soviet Union (now Russia) and its allies (countries that were under its control) were very hostile to the USA and its allies. There was a danger of war erupting and, though it did not happen, both sides were suspicious and unfriendly to each other.

- When people left Poland during the Cold War, they were not allowed to take out jewelry, works of art or money. But those who cherished objects as family heirlooms or wanted to sell them to have some money to live on found ways of doing this.

- Communism was a system where most of the buildings and workplaces were owned by the government rather than private individuals. Many people believed that would reduce the gap between rich and poor: everyone would be treated equally. Education and hospitals were free and everybody had work. Unfortunately, this didn't work out in Poland. The high-ranking officials were privileged. They bought luxury goods like meat, champagne, Belgian chocolate, caviar and oranges in special shops where you had to pay in dollars. Those who didn't have foreign money couldn't go there. Ordinary citizens often stood for hours in long queues outside grocers and meat shops and bought what was available, which often amounted to very little. Education was free but you weren't allowed to disagree with the teachers. Hospitals were also free, but neglected, and you had to bring your own sheets to make sure you lay on something clean.

- Oscar Schindler was a German man who saved the lives of 1,200 Jews during the Holocaust by giving them a job in his factory during World War II. This way they avoided starving to death or being killed by the Nazis in concentration camps.

- **Cześć** is pronounced as *Cheyshch*.
  Cz – is pronounced as ch (eg. children),
  but **ś** as a soft sh (eg. shimmer)
  and **ć** as a soft ch (eg. chin)

- The reason why migrants could not work in their professions after arriving in Australia was because their qualifications were not recognized here. Once they were proficient in English, they had to sit the Australian exams. Often after arriving in Australia, they had to work and could not afford to go to English classes.

- Once we left Poland, my parents felt safe to tell me the radio program they listened to was called 'Free Europe'. It was broadcast in Polish from London. It was illegal to listen to this station and the government interfered by overlaying it with static but it was the only way people could learn the truth about what was happening in Poland. They didn't want me to know that they were listening to something that was forbidden.

- Those further interested in the life of children behind in the Iron Curtain might also enjoy the author's animated video, *Innocence*. In *Innocence* a little girl's high spirits are in marked contrast to the somber background of post-war Warsaw, where propaganda statues create a sense of security, standing watch over her. Her love and devotion to Stalin ends suddenly, shattering her illusion. It can be found here: https://vimeo.com/355466459.

www.ingramcontent.com/pod-product-compliance
Lightning Source LLC
Chambersburg PA
CBHW071106090426
42737CB00013B/2502